One at a Time

Leslie Bulion
Illustrated by Janet Wilson

William Taylor

STECK-VAUGHN
Harcourt Supplemental Publishers

www.steck-vaughn.com

Contents

Chapter 1

Marcus Three Points

"You didn't touch your dinner, Marcus. Are you sure you're not hungry?" Dad asked.

"I never eat before a game," I said. My stomach felt like it was tied in one big knot. I took a step, jumped, and pretended to make a shot with my basketball. Then I looked out the kitchen window. "Where are they?" I asked for the third time.

"Don't worry, Marcus. They'll be here." Dad finished drying the last dish. "Your brother never misses your games, and little James has to see every minute of them." James is my five-year-old nephew.

"It's the championship game, Dad. It's the most important game of the year," I said. "I don't even think Reggie is home from work."

I went into the living room and looked out the window. Next door, my brother's house was dark. Where were Reggie's wife, Carol, and my five-year-old nephew, James? I walked around in circles.

Mom came downstairs. She had her Blue Dragons team shirt on. "Marcus, you're going to wear a path in the floor," she said.

"Sorry." I sat down and tapped my feet.

I heard Dad call out "Hey there!" I ran to the kitchen. Carol was coming in the back door. James let go of her hand and jumped into my arms.

"How did you grow so big in one day?" I asked. I pretended that he was so heavy I might drop him.

James wrapped his little arms around my neck and hung on tightly. "I ate all of my dinner," he told me.

I hugged him and took a deep breath. James always had this great little-kid smell—part fresh air and part new sneakers.

"Where's my hello from the great Marcus Three Points?" Carol asked.

I gave her a kiss.

"Daddy told me you get three points because you shoot the ball from so far away," James said.

I looked over my nephew's shoulder into the night. Reggie's white truck, with *Bidwell Builders* lettered in red, wasn't out there.

"Reggie's late," Carol said. "I thought we'd better come over anyway."

Just then the telephone rang. I picked it up and said "Hello?"

"Marcus, I'm glad I caught you." It was Reggie. "Are Carol and James there?"

"Yes, and we've got to go! Where are you, Reggie?" I asked.

"I'm a few hours away, near Welton. A friend of mine is giving me lumber from a house he's tearing down. I had to come and pick it up tonight. I'm sorry, Marcus."

I put James down. "You mean you're not coming to the game?" I couldn't believe what I was hearing. "You're not coming at all? I'm the starting center!"

"I know, and I'm proud of you, little brother," Reggie said. "James can't wait to see you out there. He really looks up to you."

"This isn't about James." I raised my voice. "It's about you being there for me."

"I am, Marcus. You know that. I want to hear every play of your game when we get together tomorrow," Reggie said. "We're still going to work on that swing set, right? You, me, and James?"

"James can't do it," I said. "He's just a kid." Carol came and stood next to me. I handed her the phone. "Reggie's not coming," I said. "I'm leaving."

I banged the kitchen door behind me and ran toward the school. So what if Reggie thought pieces of wood were more important than my championship game? Lots of other people would yell "Marcus Three Points" when I made my shots.

As I ran I felt snow on my face, but it had stopped by the time I got to school. It looked like the big storm everyone was worried about would miss our town after all. I pushed open the door to the gym. My team was already warming up.

"Marcus!" My friend Kevin threw me a basketball. I passed it back to him so hard that he had to drop it. "Take it easy," Kevin said.

"You take it easy," I said. I looked around the gym and saw Kevin's whole family sitting in the front row of the stands. I ran around the gym two times, but it didn't change how I felt.

My family came in a little later and sat in the third row—everyone except my brother. If my championship game mattered to him at all, he'd be here.

The whistle blew to start the game. The ball was tossed into the air between the other team's starting center and me. I hit the jump ball so hard it went into the stands.

"Easy, Bidwell," my coach told me.

I made two three-point shots right away. I kept going after the ball as hard as I could. I grabbed a player's arm and got called for a foul. The other team got a free shot. Right after that I fouled again.

"Watch it, Bidwell," my coach said.

I didn't care. I ran into a player on the other team and got my third foul.

"Bidwell! Cool down on the bench!" the coach yelled.

I sat down with Kevin and the rest of my team at the side of the court and waited for the coach to put me back in the game.

"What's up with you?" Kevin asked.

"Nothing," I snapped and looked away.

I saw Reggie's friend Chen standing at the door of the gym. Chen was a police captain. He was holding his radio out in front of him and just looking at it. It gave me a bad feeling. I watched him walk up into the stands with slow, heavy steps. Then he stopped in front of my family.

Chapter 2

Chen's News

My family followed Chen out of the gym. I ran after them. Mom and Dad were standing in the hall next to Carol. She held James by the hand. I leaned against the wall behind them.

Chen took off his captain's hat and pulled it around and around in his hands. Finally he looked up at us. "The storm missed this part of the state, but it's snowing hard in Welton," he began. He stopped and shook his head.

The yellow hall suddenly seemed dark. I felt like I couldn't breathe.

"Go on, Chen," Dad said. He put one arm around Carol and the other around Mom.

"Reggie was driving home from Welton. A big van slid across the road in the snow and crashed into his truck." Chen looked down again. I saw a tear splash onto his hat. "Reggie didn't make it," he whispered.

Carol grabbed Dad. She looked like she was going to fall down.

"My boy!" Mom cried. "Not my boy!"

James reached out to me. I closed my eyes and turned away.

Reggie's funeral was two days later. I didn't want to go, but I knew I had to. There was lots of talk about what a great person Reggie was. He was a good son, a kind friend, and such a wonderful father, people said.

Well, he wasn't such a great brother. A great brother wouldn't have missed his little brother's championship basketball game just to get a bunch of lumber. A great brother wouldn't have gotten himself killed.

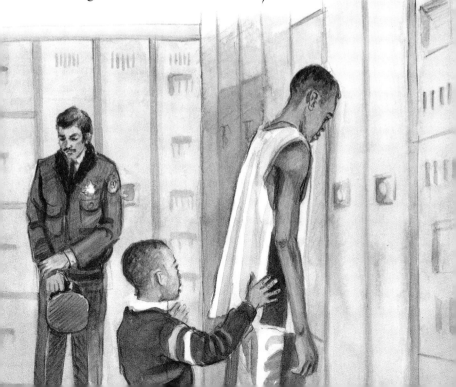

After the funeral, all of our friends and family came to our house. People kept trying to hug me and tell me how sorry they were about Reggie. There was food all over the place. The smell of it was making me sick. I backed out of the living room and ran up to my room.

I lay on my bed and stared out the window. The voices downstairs mixed together in waves of noise. None of it seemed real. I felt like I was watching a bad movie.

All I'd had on my mind for weeks was my big championship game. Now I couldn't even remember playing. At the funeral, Kevin had told me that the coaches had stopped the game as soon as they'd heard the news about Reggie.

As I lay on the bed, I went over and over Reggie's phone call in my mind. "I'm proud of you, little brother," he'd said to me that night. If he was really so proud of me, he would have been at my game. Why couldn't Reggie have stayed in town?

My thoughts were one big jumble, just like the voices downstairs. That night had been the last time I'd ever talked to my brother. I'd said some things I could never take back. I kept remembering the sound of my angry voice.

I heard someone knock softly on my door. "I'm okay," I called out. "I'm just resting."

The door opened slowly. James stood in the doorway. He came over and sat on the edge of my bed. His legs swung back and forth and he folded his hands in his lap. "There's too many people down there," he said. "I'm lonely."

I didn't want to hear that. I had known Reggie all seventeen years of my life. He was my only brother. I missed him so much I could hardly breathe. James had a mother. It was Carol's job to help James get through all of this, not mine.

"You'd better go and find your mother," I told him.

"She says that Daddy will always be my daddy," James said. He looked at his hands and pushed one thumb against the other.

I knew I should say something to help my nephew, but I just couldn't. It felt like there was something stuck in my chest. I turned over and faced the wall.

"Mama says you'll always be my uncle," James said.

Right. Just like Reggie was always supposed to be my brother. I didn't say anything. After a while, James climbed down from my bed and left. I hoped no one else would come in and try to talk to me. ⚡

Chapter 3

Reggie's Way

On Saturday morning, Mom came into my room. "Marcus, I think you should try to go back to school on Monday," she said. She held my chin in her hand and looked into my face. There were more lines around her eyes since Reggie's accident. "I know you're hurting, but you can't stay in your room forever."

I pulled my face away. I wasn't ready to go back to school. Even though I wasn't the same person I used to be, I didn't want everyone acting like I was someone special. I didn't want them to feel sorry for me.

"It's warmer out today," Mom said. "Why don't you go out and shoot some hoops?"

"I'm not playing basketball anymore," I told her. I never wanted to go back to my high school gym.

"Honey, your team is counting on you," Mom said. Her words were soft but her face was set. "You're the starting center and you can't let them down."

Why not? Reggie let me down. Everybody lets everybody down.

"Come on. Just try it," Mom said. I didn't want to, but I followed her downstairs. She opened the back door and I walked outside.

"You'll feel better after you play for a while," she said. "You'll see."

I picked up the basketball and just stood there. I looked at the kitchen window. How long did I have to stay out here?

William Taylor

My first shot missed the hoop, hitting the garage door with a bang. I threw the ball again and again, slamming it into the garage door. I didn't even try to make a shot. The ball hit the wall above the net, bounced, and sailed back over my head toward Reggie's yard. When I turned to go and get it, there was James.

"Here, Uncle Marcus," he said, holding out the ball. "Can I play with you?"

"You're too little to play basketball," I told him. I took my ball and went back to my driveway.

I started dribbling the ball up and down. I set up for a good three-point shot and missed. I dribbled, shot, and missed again. Mom was wrong. Playing basketball was not making me feel better.

"Look, Uncle Marcus," James called. "Mama said I could show you this."

James was standing beside his driveway, holding a toy ship. It was the kind you make out of pieces that snap together.

"I built this with Daddy," he said. "He showed me how."

Big deal. I took another shot and the ball bounced off the rim of the basket. I grabbed the ball and slammed it against the garage door as hard as I could. It came back at my chest so fast that it almost knocked the wind out of me.

"I'm going to get something else to show you," James called.

I heard a noise like a thump but I wasn't really listening. I dribbled the ball a few times, then I looked up at the hoop. All of a sudden, I saw my sweet spot. It was the perfect place for me to aim the basketball.

Something clicked in my head and I bent my knees without even thinking. The ball sailed up and over the basket's rim. It seemed to hang in the air for a second or two before going in. It was all net, just the way Reggie had taught me.

I closed my eyes and thought about my brother. I could see Reggie building that toy ship with little James. Reggie had a patient way of doing things, one piece at a time. He had shown me how to do lots of things that same way. It was the way he'd taught me how to play basketball.

He'd started with dribbling. Next we'd worked on how to move the ball around the basketball court. He'd shown me how to stay close to the other player to keep him from shooting or passing the ball. When I wanted to take a shot, he had taught me to bend my knees and aim for that sweet spot.

I'd had 17 years to learn things from my brother. He had died in an accident, and I could never change that. James was only five, though. He still needed Reggie, and I could do something about that. I could teach my nephew things the way that Reggie would have taught him. I could teach James the way my brother had taught me—patiently, one piece at a time.

I turned around to look for James. He wasn't near his driveway anymore. I looked across the yard next door, and saw that the basement door was open. Then I heard a crash.

Chapter 4

Coming Through

"James!" I shouted. I raced across our yards and down his basement steps. I could hear the dishwasher going in the kitchen, and I knew that Carol probably hadn't heard the crash downstairs.

After being outside in the sun, I couldn't see much of anything. "James!" I called again.

"Uncle Marcus?" James's voice sounded thin and small.

"I'm here, James. Where are you?" I tripped over a pail and fell into a pile of lumber.

"I can't get my leg out," James said.

Now I could see some shapes in the dim light. James was in the corner. Some long pieces of wood had spilled into a jumble on the floor. It looked like he was pinned by the bottom board.

I jumped over the pile of wood and moved the board off my nephew. He put his thin, little arms around my neck and I picked him up.

"Are you okay?" I asked. I sat down with James on my lap and looked at his leg. He showed me that he could straighten and bend it, and I didn't see any cuts.

"It doesn't hurt," he said. He looked more scared than anything.

"What were you doing down here?" I asked. "This isn't the greatest place for you to play."

"I wanted to show you what Daddy made for the top of my swing set." He pointed to something round in the pile of wood. It looked like a ship's wheel. "My swing set was going to be a pirate ship," he said sadly.

The ship's wheel my brother had built was beautiful. Each piece was perfect, put together with care and love. I knew then that some things about Reggie would live forever.

James had lost so much in that accident. He wouldn't even begin to understand some of it for a long, long time. No matter what had happened, though, I was still James's uncle. That was forever, too.

I hugged James and breathed in his great little-kid smell. "Your swing set will be a pirate ship," I told him.

Just then Carol came down the stairs from the kitchen. Even in the dim light of the basement, I could see how tired she looked.

"What are you doing down here?" she asked James in a worried voice. "You told me when I started filling the dishwasher that you were just going to show Uncle Marcus your ship."

"He did," I said. I stood up, still holding James. "He showed me his toy ship, and then he showed me his other ship."

Carol put her hands up to her face and rubbed her eyes. "That's right," she said. "The swing set was supposed to be a pirate ship."

"When can we start building it, Mama?" James asked.

"I don't know, James." Carol sighed. "I helped Daddy build lots of things, but I've never built a whole swing set on my own."

"You're not on your own," I told her. "You've got James. He's going to learn how to do a lot of it."

I set James down. He straightened his shoulders and stood up tall.

"You've got me, too. I know how Reggie wanted to build this," I said. "I'm going to help you and James."

Carol took both of my hands. "Your brother would be so proud of you, Marcus," she said.

"I want him to be," I said. I turned to James. "Now let's go shoot some hoops!"